Going into Space

Carmel Reilly

Contents

Space	2	Working in Space	18
Space in History	4	Resting in Space	24
Becoming an Astronaut	8	Back to Earth	28
Gravity	10	Space Fun	30
Living in Space	12	Glossary	32

Space

What would it be like to go into space?
What would it be like to see the Moon up close?

Some people have been to space. Some have walked on the Moon. There are even some people who are living in space right now!

Big Stars
Stars are huge! They only look tiny because they are very far away. Our Sun is a star. You could fit 1.4 million Earths inside the Sun.

Space in History

Thousands of years ago, people used the Sun, Moon, stars and **planets** to work out how to tell the time and the months of the year.

An ancient **astronomer** looks up at the stars.

Going to Space

In the 1950s, **scientists** made rockets that went into space. Space travel is very dangerous, so the first rockets went to space without people on them.

This rocket was launched in 1958.

Laika

The very first space traveller was a dog called Laika. She was sent to space in a rocket in 1957.

The first **astronauts** travelled in rockets. Today, they travel in space shuttles.

A space rocket

In 1961, Yuri Gagarin became the first person to travel to space.

In 1969, Neil Armstrong became the first person to walk on the Moon.

Space in the Future

Space is a very, very big place. So far, people have been to a very small part of it. Astronauts have never been to other planets.

A space shuttle

Mars

The closest planet to Earth is Mars. Astronauts hope to go there by 2035.

Becoming an Astronaut

Becoming an astronaut is hard work. Astronauts have to study very hard at school and university.

Astronauts learn how to fly the Space Shuttle.

Then they spend many years learning about space travel, the Space Shuttle and the special **equipment** on board. They also have to be very fit and healthy.

Scientists make sure that astronauts are fit and healthy.

Accidents

Space travel can be dangerous.
More than twenty astronauts
have died in accidents.

In 1986, the Space Shuttle
Challenger exploded.
Sadly, all astronauts
on board died.

Gravity

Gravity is what makes things fall to the ground. In space, there is very little gravity, so nothing falls. Everything just floats around – even people!

Astronauts are taller in space than they are on Earth. There is less gravity pulling down on their bodies.

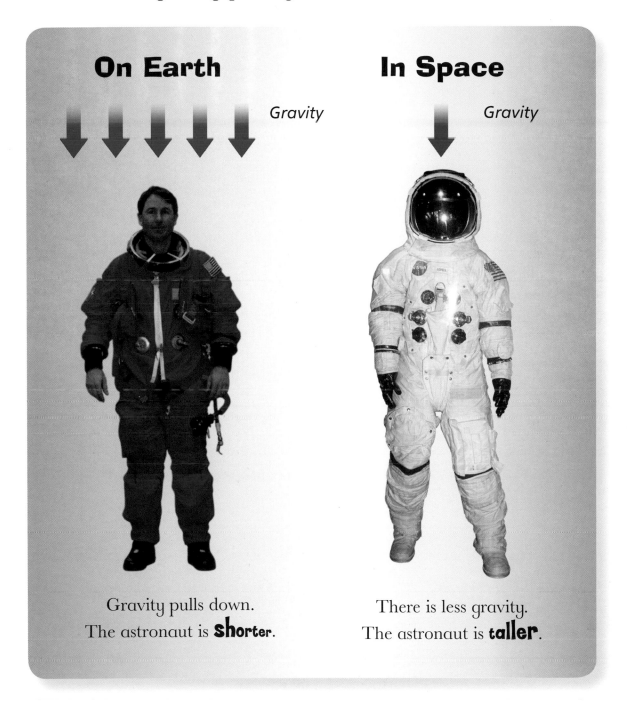

On Earth

Gravity

Gravity pulls down.
The astronaut is **shorter**.

In Space

Gravity

There is less gravity.
The astronaut is **taller**.

Living in Space

When astronauts finish their training, they go on space missions. Some of these missions are short, but some can last for weeks or even months.

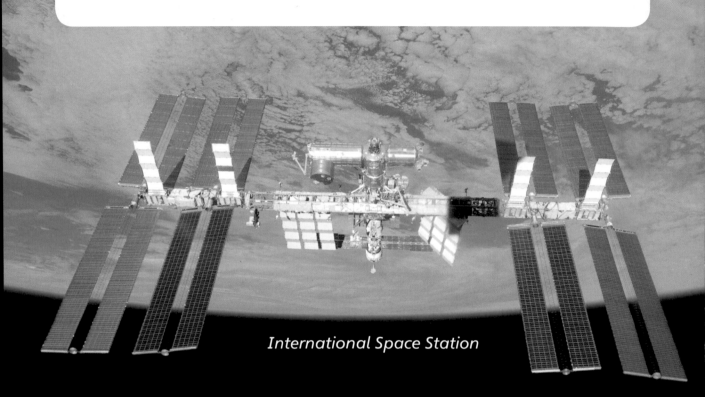

International Space Station

Space Stations

Astronauts on long **missions** live on the **International Space Station**.

In the International Space Station

Kitchen
- microwaves
- refrigerators
- water
- frozen food. Most of the food is cooked on Earth and frozen. Astronauts just have to re-heat it.

Bedrooms
- special beds to stop the astronauts from floating while they sleep
- computers
- lockers, to store clothes and other personal items

Bathroom
- toilet
- towels
- wet wipes and cloths, for washing

Gym
- treadmill
- exercise bike

Laboratories
- machines, equipment and tools to carry out scientific experiments
- computers

Eating in Space

Imagine trying to eat when your food won't stay on the plate and your water won't stay in the cup! That's what it's like when astronauts try to eat and drink in space.

An astronaut watches some water floating.

Space Food

In the early days of space travel, an astronaut's food came in tubes, like toothpaste!

Watch Out for Those Crumbs!

Astronauts must make sure that bits of food, water and other rubbish do not float around the space station. Even the smallest crumbs could damage the equipment.

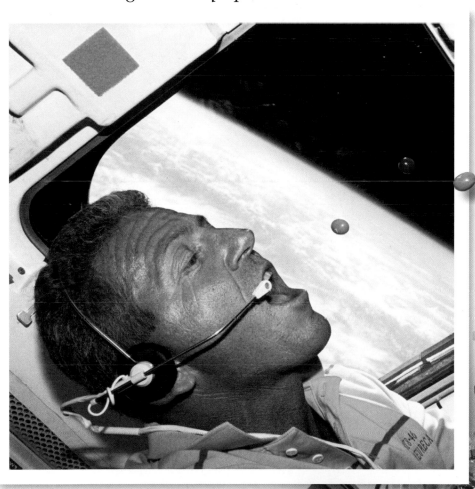

Eating chocolates and biscuits in space!

Keeping Clean in Space

Astronauts don't take showers because the water would just float away. So they use wet cloths and wipes to keep clean.

Space Toilets!

The Space Station has special toilets that suck waste safely away.

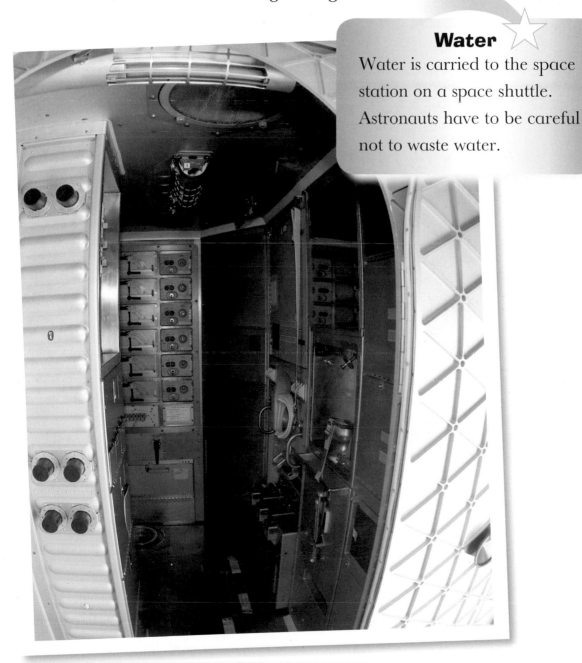

All the waste produced at the Space Station is stored and taken back to Earth.

Working in Space

Astronauts don't go to space for a holiday! Each astronaut has important work to do.

Experiments

Astronauts look at how living in space affects their bodies. They also take plants into space and see how living in space affects them.

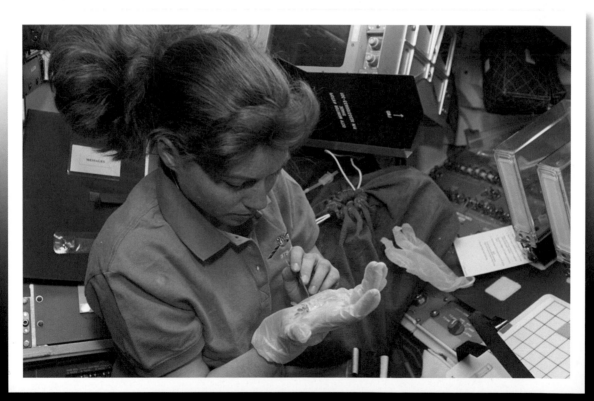

This astronaut is doing an experiment on a plant.

Astronauts also watch Earth from space. This helps them to learn more about things that happen on Earth, like fires or floods.

This astronaut is taking photos of space.

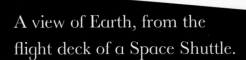

A view of Earth, from the flight deck of a Space Shuttle.

Walking in Space

Sometimes, parts of the Space Station need to be fixed. So astronauts have to go outside the Space Station. They walk in space!

This astronaut is working outside the Space Station.

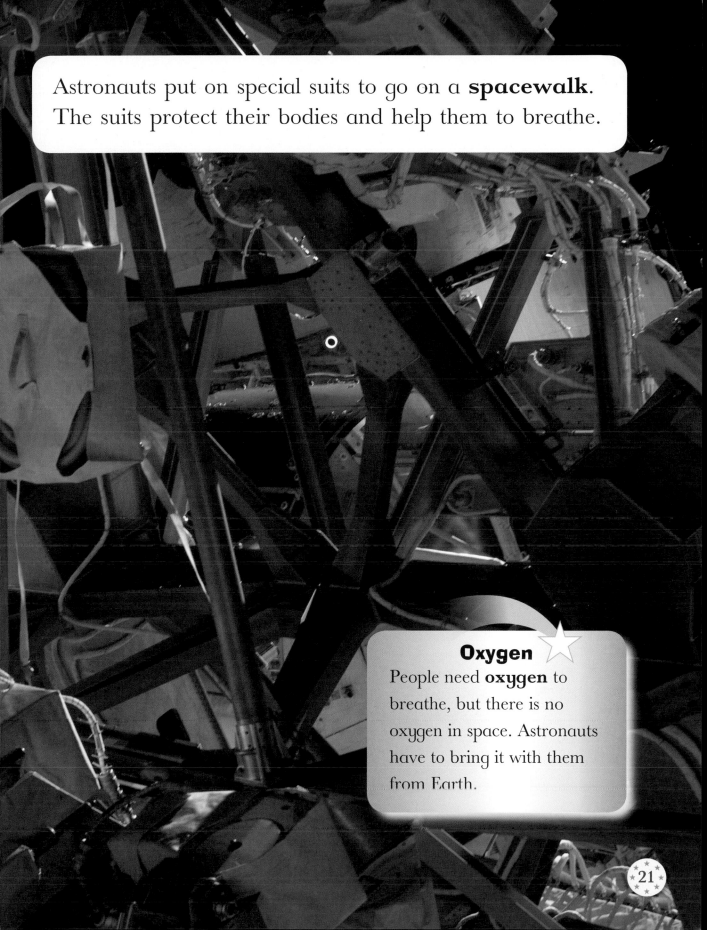

Astronauts put on special suits to go on a **spacewalk**. The suits protect their bodies and help them to breathe.

Oxygen

People need **oxygen** to breathe, but there is no oxygen in space. Astronauts have to bring it with them from Earth.

Spacesuits

oxygen tanks:
carry the oxygen

**earphones
and microphone:**
*let astronauts talk
to each other*

helmet:
*protects the head
and makes sure
there is oxygen
for the astronaut
to breathe*

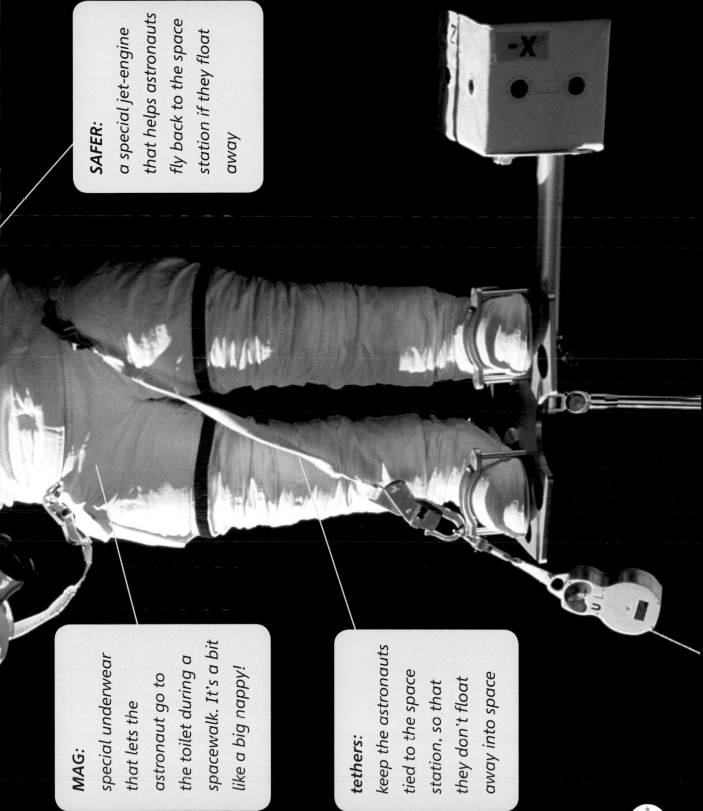

Resting in Space

Astronauts work hard in the space station,
but they also need to relax and take care of their bodies.

Reading in space.

Exercise

In space, astronauts exercise a lot. Back on Earth, gravity helps to keep our muscles and bones strong. In space, astronauts have to exercise more to make sure their bones and muscles stay strong.

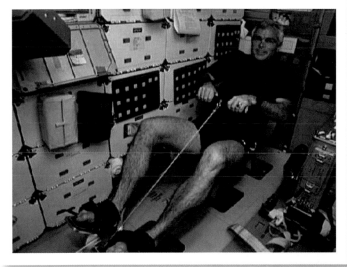

Exercising in space.

Fitness training in space.

Sleep

Sleeping in space is not easy. Astronauts have to be tied into sleeping bags to stop them floating away while they sleep!

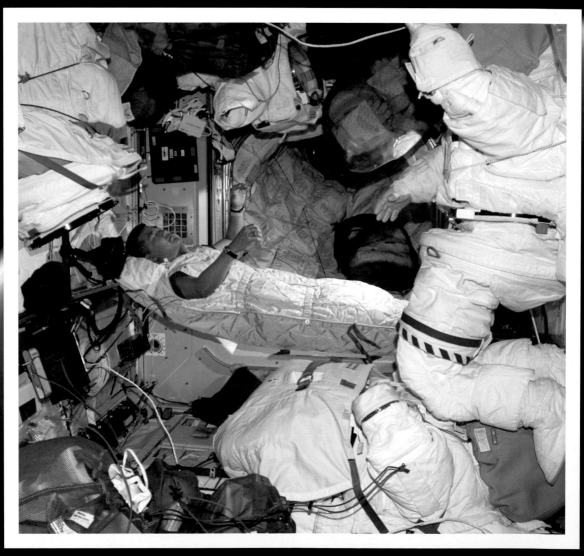

This astronaut is sleeping.

Day and Night, Night and Day

Days on the Space Station are much shorter than days on Earth. The sun rises and sets every 90 minutes. This can make it hard to get a good night's sleep. By the time you drop off to sleep, it is morning again!

Sun

Earth

Back to Earth

When astronauts have finished their mission, they take the Space Shuttle back to Earth.

The Space Shuttle flies towards Earth.

The Space Shuttle flies towards the landing strip.

After months in space, astronauts must learn how to live on Earth again. They may have forgotten what it's like to live with gravity. It can even be difficult for them to walk at first.

The back wheels touch down.

A parachute slows down the Shuttle. The Shuttle has landed!

Going to space is fantastic – but it's always nice to come home again!

Space Fun

Space Spotting

Spot the four differences between these astronauts.

Answers

1. Red lens on camera
2. Missing NASA badge
3. Missing red band on leg
4. Missing black dot on bottom of jet pack

Space Quiz

How much do you remember?

1. Have human beings walked on the Moon?

2. Which planet is closest to Earth?

3. Are astronauts taller on Earth or in space?

4. What makes objects fall to the ground on Earth?

5. How do astronauts wash themselves in space?

Glossary

astronaut
person who pilots a spacecraft or works in space

astronomer
person who studies objects in space

equipment
machines and tools that help people do their work

experiments
tests that help people learn more about the world

gravity
force by which a planet pulls objects towards its centre

International Space Station
large satellite that orbits Earth. It is large enough for several astronauts to live and work in

missions
tasks or jobs that astronauts are sent on

oxygen
gas that humans breathe to live

planets
objects in space that orbit around a star

scientists
people who study and learn about the world around them

spacesuit
special outfit worn by astronauts to protect them in space

spacewalk
when an astronaut moves and works in space outside the Space Station or Space Shuttle